MW01602160

Paws For a Moment

A book about companionship and reconnecting with yourself.

This includes 30 days of activities to inspire your soul while

connecting with your favorite puppy!

Written By:
Neal J. Gyles

Published By:
PAWS MOMENT LLC
Leominster, MA

Introduction

Why We Paws

We're exposed to so many elements throughout our day —

noise, pressure, distractions.

Sometimes, we just forget to be.

But dogs don't forget.

They live in the moment.

They listen with their eyes.

They love with their whole body.

They feel us, even when we can't feel ourselves.

This book is your invitation to slow down and appreciate the

beautiful bond right in front of you.

Not to train your dog, but to learn from them.

When we take even just 15 minutes to truly pause,

we start to see things differently.

Ourselves. Our habits. Our hearts.

This book is here to remind you of the love you deserve.

Paws for a Moment: Mindful Bonding Between You and Your Dog

Copyright © 2025 Neal Gyles

Published by Paws Moment LLC
www.pawsmoment.com

This book is for educational and inspirational purposes only and is not intended to serve as medical or veterinary advice. Always consult a qualified professional for concerns about you or your dog's health.

Printed in the United States of America

First Edition

ISBN: 9798284065051
Imprint: Independently published

How to experience the Paws

Each day offers three simple parts:

Pawsitive Insight: A powerful truth about your dog's behavior or the bond you share.

Activity: A playful or meaningful moment to try with your dog, something that brings the insight to life.

Paws for a Moment: A gentle reflection to help you grow, connect, and see yourself through your dog's eyes.

It's simple.

It takes just 15 minutes.

One day at a time.

Be present. Be curious. Be open.

You don't have to get it perfect.

You just have to show up.

Day 1: Eye Contact is Everything

Pawsitive Insight

Eye contact is one of the most powerful forms of connection in the animal world. Almost no species use it the way dogs do. Unlike wolves, who see direct eye contact as a challenge, dogs evolved to hold it softly, steadily, and with purpose.

When your pup looks into your eyes, their brain releases oxytocin (the love hormone)—it's also the same hormone that bonds infants to their parents. Your brain does the same in return. Over thousands of years, dogs didn't just learn to live with us; they rewired their biology to love us with their eyes.

The Look of Love

Sit with your dog at their level and try to meet their eyes.

No commands. Just be there. Stay close, stay calm, and let them feel your energy.

When it happens, even for a second, you'll both feel it.

Paws for a Moment

Most people spend their lives trying to be seen. We change ourselves, filter ourselves just to feel noticed, accepted, and loved.

Today, you didn't have to do anything. You didn't have to impress. You didn't even have to speak. You let yourself be in the moment, and you were seen.

No judgment. No pressure. Just love.

Day 2: Jealous? More Like Bonding

Pawsitive Insight

Dogs can feel protective of your attention — not in a possessive way, but in a bonded way.

When you show affection to another dog, stare too long at a screen, or give your energy elsewhere, they notice.

And sometimes, they respond — stepping in, nudging you, reminding you that they're still right there.

It's not drama. It's connection.

They don't want all your energy — they just want to know they haven't been forgotten in the overflow.

Stop. In the Name of the Paw.

Now its time to stop everything and focus your attention on the cutest one in the room. Let your pup know they're your main priority and give them a moment to remember. I'm talking barrel rolls through the living room. Run away like they're trying to rob you. This is the moment they been waiting for all day.

Paws for a Moment

Your dog doesn't hold grudges.

But they notice when the space between you grows.

They don't know what's on your mind.

They just know when they've lost your presence.

Have you been distracted lately?

What's one small thing you could sacrifice daily… to make living in the now feel like enough?

Day 3: I've Been Watching

Pawsitive Insight

Dogs are capable of something called social learning, a powerful cognitive ability where they observe and imitate human behavior without being directly taught.

In controlled studies, dogs successfully completed tasks like opening containers, pressing levers, or retrieving hidden objects simply by watching a human demonstrate the action.

This tells us that dogs aren't just trained by commands but they're shaped by visual learning. They learn from your posture, your habits, your mood, and how you interact with the world.

Do It Like This

Create a little "observation setup" today using objects from around your home. Stack three cardboard boxes or bins with an easy-to-open lid. Place a treat or toy under one. Let your dog see it. Then slowly lift the box to reveal it and do it again with a second and third variation. No commands. No words.

Now mix up the stack, take a step back, and let your dog try.

Notice what they remember and how much they learn just by being near you.

Paws for a Moment

You may not realize it yet, but someone admires you.

They admire the way you move through this world.

Take a moment. Take a breath.

And take a good look at what they see.

Admire yourself.

Day 4: Just Fifteen

Pawsitive Insight

Play is a full-body release. In recent studies, just 15 minutes of unstructured play between a dog and their person measurably reduced stress, lowered heart rate, and improved mood for both of you.

This isn't exercise. It's not obedience. It's presence in motion.

Play turns off the parts of your brain stuck in control and activates the ones wired for joy.

We're Under Attack!

This is not a drill. You are under siege.

Construct your stronghold using pillows, blankets, and whatever supplies can be gathered from the living room battlefield. Your dog's base? Equally fortified… or at least fluffed. Once in position, the games begin. Launch plush projectiles, defend your walls with honor, and prepare for chaos.

Your dog may charge in like an orc from the wild lands — eyes wide, paws thundering, tail a blur. If they freeze instead, rally the spirit with a mighty "TAKE COVER!" and resume battle.

This is a legendary standoff between beasts and bellies.

This is a victory measured in drool.

Paws for a Moment

Time goes by so quick.

And with your pup, it goes by even faster.

It just takes 15 minutes to activate joy.

That's all it takes. Just 15 minutes.

Day 5: I Know That Face

Pawsitive Insight

Dogs don't just recognize your scent or voice — they can identify your face visually, even in photographs.

In controlled studies using screens and still images, dogs consistently responded more to photos of their owners than to unfamiliar faces. They showed increased focus, body language shifts, and even signs of emotional response — without needing scent, sound, or movement.

This puts them in rare company. Most animals, even intelligent ones, struggle with facial recognition in photos. But your dog? They can pick you out of a pile of strangers because your face means home.

This Is Me

Pull out a few old photos of yourself — as a kid, a teen, and now. Lay them out in front of your pup like you're showing them your origin story.

Narrate it if you want:

"That's me when I was little."

"That's who I was back then."

Now point to yourself: "And this is me now."

Let them sniff, paw, tilt their head. Let them see the timeline and the person they've anchored to.

Paws for a Moment

You've grown. You've changed.

But your pup doesn't need the backstory.

They just love the person in front of them.

They get a short window in your life.

You get their whole lifetime.

What are you doing to make it beautiful?

Day 6: What's That Smell? Is That Stress?

Pawsitive Insight

Dogs don't just sense your stress, they smell it. Research shows dogs can detect changes in your body odor and breath when you're anxious or under pressure. What's more, their own stress hormones can rise in response. That means your inner world doesn't stay hidden. To your dog, it has a scent. Their body reacts to your emotions as if they're happening to them too because in a way, they are. You and your dog aren't just emotionally close, you're biologically linked.

Bark It Out

Grab a pillow, look at your dog, and say something silly like, "Okay, we're getting this stress OUT." Shake your arms and legs while your dog watches (they might even join in!). Then bury your face in the pillow and let out a scream, a groan, or a deep sigh. Yes, it'll feel ridiculous. But studies show that this kind of vocal release, known as somatic discharge, helps reset the nervous system and lower cortisol. It mirrors how animals instinctively shake off stress. You're not being dramatic. You're being honest. And your dog? They'll understand.

Once you've let it out, sit with your pup. Breathe slowly. Speak softly. Pet them with presence. Let them smell the shift in you.

Let calm become something you create together.

Paws for a Moment

They already know when something's wrong. They feel it in their body. You don't have to hide your anxiety. You just have to meet it with care. When you regulate yourself, you regulate them. This is how peace becomes a shared language.

Let that stress out, for them.

And more importantly, for you.

Day 7: The Beat of Your Heart

Pawsitive Insight

In moments of calm bonding, a dog's heart rhythm can naturally align with their human's. A phenomenon that researchers have observed during quiet, emotionally attuned interactions like resting or gentle touch.

This physiological mirroring, sometimes called cardiac synchrony, isn't conscious or trained. It's a byproduct of co-regulation — when two nervous systems recognize safety and respond in sync.

It's not just your dog relaxing near you. It's your bodies speaking the same language of calm, without a single word exchanged.

Heart to Heart

Set the scene: low lights, quiet space, maybe your favorite playlist on in the background.

Now stretch out next to your floof — your pup, your sidekick, your four-legged roommate.

Place your hand gently on their chest or belly. Breathe slowly. Notice their rhythm. Let yours settle with theirs.

If your pup lets out that deep, cozy sigh? That's the good stuff.

Paws for a Moment

Your heart syncs up with your pup and you feel the magic.

It's the kind of connection we forget to be grateful for.

When was the last time you stopped and appreciated how beautiful your heart really is?

Day 8: I Forgive You, For What Again?

Pawsitive Insight

Dogs aren't wired to judge you the way humans do.

They don't recognize "flaws" the way we do. They don't care if you've gained weight, messed up, or are holding shame you haven't told anyone about. What they read is your energy, the consistency of your presence, your tone, your affection, and your scent. To them, that is you, and if you've ever worried you weren't enough, your dog has already disagreed. With every tail wag, every snuggle, every time they followed you from room to room just to stay near the real version of you.

But I Love You Tho

Sit down with your dog and tell them one thing you've been embarrassed about. Something you've judged yourself for — your body, your fear, your past. Say it out loud. Then look at them. Watch how they don't flinch. They don't turn away. They don't change. They'll probably just wag or lick your hand.

Let that moment sink in. They already forgave the thing that you haven't. They already loved the part you're trying to hide.

Paws for a Moment

Maybe the part of you that feels hardest to love

is the part your dog accepts the most.

They don't need you to be better.

They just need you to be you.

So if you ever forget who you are,

look into the eyes of the one who never did.

Day 9: The Scent That Stays

Pawsitive Insight

Your dog doesn't just remember your routines, they remember you. Even after years apart, dogs have been known to recognize a beloved human's scent instantly, showing signs of joy, excitement, and emotional familiarity.

Their noses are strong enough to detect a single part per trillion but it's not just about strength. It's about significance. When your scent means safety, comfort, love, and they remember it for life.

Leave a Little Love Behind

Let's put together a trail of remembrance for your fluff.

Take an old shirt you've worn a thousand times — the one that basically is you now.

Your scent is baked into it. And to them, that scent means everything. Wrap it in a bag or box. Turn it into a gift. This isn't just fabric, it's comfort they can hold.

Leave it where they sleep, hide it in their bed, or place it somewhere quiet. It's a reminder that you're still here, even when you're not.

Paws for a Moment

It's not just an old shirt.

It's your laugh. Your comfort. Your entire existence captured in a single whiff.

That scent unlocks something they never question, love.

They won't forget you. Not today. Not ever.

Day 10: I've Never Seen That One Before

Pawsitive Insight

Dogs aren't limited to repeating what they've been taught. In a surprising cognitive study, researchers gave dogs a cue that meant "do something different" and many responded by offering new, self-invented behaviors. These weren't random movements. They were chosen with intent.

This tells us something remarkable. When encouraged, dogs are capable of spontaneous creativity, not just imitation or obedience. They don't always need to be told what to do. Sometimes, they're waiting to be invited to try something new.

Wait... How Did You Do That?

Today, skip the commands. Instead, sit or stand in front of your dog and say your chosen cue ("Show me something new" or "Let's make something up"). Don't point or prompt. Just observe what they offer: maybe they stretch, spin, back up, or flick their paw.

Whatever they do, acknowledge it. Give a treat or praise.

Then, reinforce that move with a custom name ("That's your twirl!" or "Do the bow!"). Let them invent. Then name it.

Paws for a Moment

Most people will go day by day wishing to do that one thing they always wanted the freedom to do. Our thoughts feel like such a weight. Self-doubt is the one thing that can ruin your "do something different" moment.

Day 11: Steady Steps, Trusting Paws

Pawsitive Insight

Dogs engage in a behavior called social referencing. They look to their human for cues on how to respond to unfamiliar or ambiguous situations. This isn't obedience. It's emotional intelligence.

When something new happens, dogs don't just react — they pause and study your face, body language, and tone. If you stay relaxed, they're more likely to explore. If you freeze or tense up, they become wary.

This ability to interpret your signals in real-time is one of the clearest signs that dogs see you not just as a companion, but as their emotional guide.

Your body tells them if the world is safe.

Walk This Way, Trust Me

Choose a new place to walk your pup today — somewhere quiet but unfamiliar. As you move, pay close attention to how they scan their environment. If they hesitate, don't pull or rush. Just breathe, smile, and keep your posture relaxed. Be the steady presence they're searching for.

Paws for a Moment

You don't have to always know the next step.

But someone's watching you — not to judge, but to understand how safe the world is supposed to feel.

Your pup doesn't need you to be fearless. Just steady.

They trust you to lead through the unknown...why don't you?

Day 12: A Sniff into the Past

Pawsitive Insight

Dogs don't rely on visual memory to understand where they've been. They rely on scent. Their brains build detailed maps of the world based on scent trails, not sights or sounds.

Each time you walk through a space, you leave behind scent particles that hold information about your identity, your mood, and how long it's been since you were there. Dogs can track these trails hours later, even in environments filled with competing smells. To your dog, scent is memory, and you leave more of yourself behind than you realize.

A Whiff of Time

Pick three objects that hold your scent — something old, something new, and something worn (like a childhood stuffed animal, your favorite hoodie, and today's socks).

Place them in a triangle on the floor and let your dog explore each one without prompting.

Then sit beside them and just observe. Which do they sniff first? Which one do they stay with the longest? Which one makes them relax?

Paws for a Moment

Today, your dog wandered through your past and present.

A soft trail of who you've been, and who you are.

They didn't judge the worn-out parts.

They didn't favor the newest version.

They stayed close to whatever felt the most you.

Day 13: What the Tilt?

Pawsitive Insight

That adorable head tilt your dog does? It's not just for show. Studies suggest dogs tilt their heads to help process human speech, especially when they hear familiar words like their name, toy cues, or emotional tones. It helps them locate the sound, focus their attention, and understand you better. This isn't a random quirk. It's your dog saying, "I'm trying to get this right."

Tilt Talk Time

Vent. Ramble. Rant. Share the weird thing that happened this morning or the hard thing that's been sitting on your chest.

Say it all to your dog — and don't forget to throw in: "You're my best friend."

Talk like they're your therapist, your journal, your ride-or-die.

See how they respond. Do they tilt their head? Raise an eyebrow? Gaze at you like they're holding space?

Your listening buddy is right here, ready for the latest updates on your life — and they're not judging a thing.

Paws for a Moment

Even when we talk, not everyone will understand what we're going through.

But sometimes, what we really need is to listen to ourselves.

When we feel lost or unsure, our emotions can feel tilted, like they're pointing in a direction we can't quite follow.

But if we speak our truth and stay with it long enough,

we realize clarity comes from one simple act of Listening.

Day 14: You Always Come Back

Pawsitive Insight

When you walk back through the door, your dog doesn't just see you, they feel you. It's called reunion joy (a behavior that reflects how deeply a dog is bonded to their human). For some dogs, it's full-body wiggles and paw storms. For others, it's quieter — a tail thump, a deep exhale, a slow head bow into your legs.

But no matter how it shows up, it's real. The moment you return is a moment they've been waiting for. The way they greet you is their personal way of saying, "I never stopped loving you while you were gone."

Mini Party, Major Love

Come home like it's a reunion. Even if you just ran to the mailbox. Walk in with a smile. Say "Hi baby!" like you mean it.

Give them 15 seconds of full presence — belly rubs, excited energy, silly nicknames. Let them know the moment you return is a moment you cherish too.

You are the party they waited for. So make it one!

Paws for a Moment

They never know how long you'll be gone.

But they believe, every time, that you'll come back.

And when you do, they don't hold back their joy.

They don't play it cool. They celebrate your return like it's the best moment of their life.

Sometimes, just showing up is the biggest joy of all.

Day 15: Pup POV

Pawsitive Insight

Dogs aren't just tuned in to how you treat them. They are watching how you treat everyone. In behavioral studies, dogs consistently avoided people who acted unkindly toward their owners, even if those same people later tried to offer them a reward. They showed preference for those who were helpful, warm, or cooperative, even in situations that didn't directly involve the dog.

This means your dog isn't only reading tone and treats. They're observing character. To them, how you show up in the world matters. This is not just for them, but for everyone around you.

Show Them Your Heart

Today, you are going to land the job of a lifetime: being your pup's role model.

Do two or three small acts of kindness on purpose. Open a door for someone. Let someone merge in traffic. Clean up something you didn't have to.

Your furry little witness is watching how you move.

Let them see the kind of human they can be proud to follow.

Paws for a Moment

They don't just follow your voice. They follow your integrity.

Your dog sees how you speak to strangers, how you move through stress, how you carry yourself when no one else is looking.

The choices you make are yours, so choose to be some one your pup is proud to love.

Day 16: In Sync

Pawsitive Insight

Dogs don't just walk next to you; they sync with you.

Behavioral research shows dogs naturally adjust their pace, direction, and even patterns of rest and movement to mirror their humans. It's not about control or training, it's about connection. Over time, your dog shapes their rhythm to yours because they want to stay with you. Not ahead. Not behind. Just with you.

Paw Step, Paw Step

Go for a long walk. This is not to get steps in or burn calories, but to notice. Pay attention to your dog's pace. Are they slowing down when you slow? Waiting when you pause? Let the leash stay loose and the pressure melt off. Try syncing your footsteps. You don't have to say a word. Just be beside them.

This isn't about direction, it's about rhythm. Rhythm is how bonds speak without words.

Paws for a Moment

The people who love us don't always pull us forward.

Sometimes, they just walk with us through the slow, the messy, the still. They adjust their steps to ours, not because they must but because staying close matters more than getting there fast.

Day 17: Get on My Level

Pawsitive Insight

The play bow is one of the clearest, most universal signals in dog behavior — chest lowered, back end raised, tail wagging. It tells other dogs, "This is play."

What's surprising is that dogs also recognize this signal when humans imitate it. Even if you're awkward or unbalanced, dogs interpret that lowered posture and bouncing energy as a clear invite to play.

They're not judging your form. They're reading your intent.

This kind of cross-species play is rare in the animal world, and it's one more way dogs show how tuned in they are to us.

Bow Down, Baby

Try it. No matter how weird it feels. Drop to your hands and knees, wiggle, crawl a little, and pop into a play bow. Let your dog see you be playful, vulnerable, and goofy. Make a noise — a bark, a howl, a squeaky.

See what they do. Most dogs will instantly respond with tail wags, bounces, zoomies, or bows of their own. This is how you say: "I'm here to play with you, on your level."

Paws for a Moment

There's a reason dogs never look embarrassed when they play.

They're not carrying ego. They're not performing.

They're just present, alive in the moment, exactly as they are.

And when we meet them there, something shifts.

Not because we're acting like a dog, but because we're finally letting go of the pressure to act like anything else.

When we stop judging ourselves for being ourselves, that's when the light of joy shines through. That's when we feel free.

Day 18: Dreaming of You

Pawsitive Insight

When dogs sleep, their brains follow the same patterns as ours. This includes REM cycles, where dreams happen. Research shows their brain activity during this stage is strikingly similar to a dreaming human. Since dogs build memories around their daily experiences and emotional bonds, it's likely their dreams include the people they love most. That twitching paw; that soft bark in their sleep. They might be chasing a ball — or running back toward you. Even in rest, you're still with them.

Dream Scene Director

Give your dog the best dream material possible. Pick out their favorite toy and play till you can't play anymore. Let them get tired in the best way. Then, when they fall asleep, narrate it like a movie:

"You're now dreaming of winning the treat lottery."

"You're getting the best sleep of your life." Be the director. You're the memory they're falling asleep with.

Paws for a Moment

You leave a bigger imprint than you think. Not just in the loud moments, but in the quiet ones that linger after.

They carry you into their sleep because you matter. Not for what you do, but for how you make them feel.

They dream about the life they love. You're in it. Are you dreaming about yours, and chasing it too?

Day 19: When Love Has a Tone

Pawsitive Insight

When dogs hear your voice, their brain responds similarly to how a human child processes a parent's tone. Research shows dogs are highly attuned to prosody (the emotional melody of speech) and can distinguish loving, excited, or soothing tones from neutral ones. This means the way you speak to your dog deeply affects how they feel, even if they don't know every word. When you speak with warmth, your dog quite literally feels loved. You're not just talking. You are shaping their emotional world.

Pupoetry

Write down your favorite moments with your pup from the moment you held them for the first time, to your little inside jokes, and all the ways they've brought joy into your life. Let it become a short, sweet poem. It doesn't have to rhyme or sound perfect, just speak from the heart. Then read it out loud to your dog. Use your most loving, silly, or soft voice. Let them hear how much they mean to you. This one's just for you two.

Paws for a Moment

"If I'd never met you, my life wouldn't be the same.

From your very first lick to the way that you came.

You've changed me in ways I'll never quite name.

You don't even know what you've done for me,

My life has become what I'm trying to be.

You painted this canvas I call my heart

The one that you helped me create, like art."

Day 20: They Feel the Empty Space Too

Pawsitive Insight

Dogs mourn the ones they've loved. They grieve the quiet after the chaos. The absence of footsteps. The missing chair. The person who doesn't walk through the door anymore.

It's been observed across homes and studies that after a loss, dogs often sleep more, pace, whine, lose interest in food, or linger in places where someone used to be.

They may not understand what happened, but they understand something's missing. They feel the shift. They feel the space.

And just like us, they hold on.

Grieve Together

If you've lost someone, a person, a pet, a chapter of your life, let your dog be part of that moment.

Sit beside them. Light a candle. Look at a photo or speak a name. Let your dog curl into your lap, lay across your feet, or just sit near you while you both remember.

You don't have to explain anything. Just be there, together.

Paws for a Moment

We grieve because we love with our whole heart.

The ache we feel now is love that no longer has a place to land.

Grief is the echo of connection.

The hurt resembles love in the most beautiful, painful way.

Grieving is not to break but to remember.

To honor that love, for the ones you've lost,

is everything they would have wanted.

Day 21: Because You're Worth It

Pawsitive Insight

Dogs are wired to enjoy comfort, but they also crave novelty, especially when it feels safe. This behavior is called neophilia (the preference for new experiences within familiar surroundings).

A new treat in a known room, a different walk route with their favorite human, and a surprise moment in a predictable day.

These tiny shifts spark joy and attention. When you create a moment that's just a little different, they notice. It doesn't have to be big. It just has to be on purpose.

Dinner for Two

Tonight, you both get your favorite meal. Order or cook something that feels like a true treat, no shortcuts, no "being good." While you're at it, get your dog something just for them: their favorite chew, a special treat, a frozen lick mat, or a homemade dog-safe dinner.

Now change the setting. Ditch the usual couch routine.

Pick a new spot, a blanket on the floor, a quiet corner of the yard and sit close. Eat together. Just you two, celebrating the moment for no reason at all.

Paws for a Moment

You don't need a holiday to do something kind for yourself.

You don't need a big win, or a rough day, or a reason that makes sense to anyone else. Sometimes the most powerful thing you can do is choose joy on purpose.

Your dog never questions why they get the treat.

They just receive it.

Day 22: When They Lean, They Love

Pawsitive Insight

When your dog leans their body weight against you — whether sitting beside you, resting their head on your lap, or pressing into your side — they're doing more than showing affection.

This behavior activates pressure-based co-regulation, which calms their nervous system. It's the same principle used in weighted blankets for anxiety, and it goes both ways. That steady contact lowers stress in both of you, syncing breath, heart rate, and emotional state.

To your dog, leaning on you is a way of saying: "I feel safe enough to let go."

Feel the Lean

Sit or lie down somewhere cozy, and let your dog naturally come to rest against you. Don't guide. Don't invite. Just be there. When they lean in, even slightly, stay still. Let the weight settle between you. This is the kind of hug dogs give without arms.

Paws for a Moment

You carry so much without asking for help.

You tighten your shoulders, steady your breath, and pretend it doesn't feel heavy. But today, you didn't have to hold it all.

Someone came close. Pressed into you.

Said with their body: "You're allowed to rest now."

Day 23: Welcome to the Snuggle Den

Pawsitive Insight

Dogs are natural den animals. In the wild, they seek enclosed spaces to rest, raise their young, and feel protected. That instinct didn't disappear with domestication, it just adapted. Most dogs still feel safest in cozy, covered environments (crates, under tables, behind couches). They're not hiding; they're regulating.

When you create an enclosed space and share it with your dog, you're speaking their primal language: "This is our safe zone. We rest here together."

To your pup, sharing a den isn't just about comfort, it's trust in its purest form.

Snuggle Shelter

Grab a blanket, some pillows, some chips and build a cozy fort.

Make it just big enough for you and your pup to crawl into.

Add a toy, a treat, or their favorite blankey.

Then get inside. Breathe. Snuggle. Be adorable!

Bonus points if you both fall asleep.

Paws for a Moment

You don't need four walls and a roof to feel safe.

Sometimes, all it takes is a blankey, a breath, and someone who says, "I've got you."

And in that little fort, you remember safety isn't a place.

It's a feeling.

Day 24: When They Bring You Joy

Pawsitive Insight

When a dog brings you a toy, they're performing a social behavior rooted in pack bonding and cooperative play. In wild canines, this kind of object-sharing helps strengthen social ties, practice hunting behaviors, and build trust within the group.

Domesticated dogs adapted this instinct not for survival, but for emotional connection. They aren't giving you the toy to get rid of it. They're offering it to engage with you, co-regulate energy, and show affection.

To your dog, play isn't a distraction, it's a relationship ritual.

Toy Parade

Let your pup pick a toy, then celebrate it like it's the greatest treasure in the world. Clap, roll around, play a little tug-of-war. Let them proudly prance around and you can join their proud parade!

If they drop it on your lap? You can say "aww," because that's not just a toy, that's trust.

Paws for a Moment

Your dog doesn't second-guess joy. They live in it.

When they offer it to you, they're not asking for anything.

They're just saying, "Come feel this with me."

When did sharing happiness start to feel like something you had to earn or explain?

Day 25: The Memory They Hold

Pawsitive Insight

Dogs possess what researchers call episodic-like memory. This means they can recall past experiences that were emotionally significant, especially those involving excitement, reward, or bonding.

Unlike habits or training routines, these memories are not triggered by repetition. They're triggered by feeling. Games like hide-and-seek activate a dog's spatial memory, problem-solving skills, and emotional center. Reinforcing not just the action, but the happiness behind it. What your dog remembers most is how you made them feel during the moment.

It's Game Time!

Give your pup a treat… and then run for the hills — or at least under the bed. Let the wild game of hide-and-seek begin.

Once you're hidden, call their name. When they find you? Cheer like it's the day they finally stopped peeing in the house.

Switch up your hiding spots. Keep the energy flowing.

Let them sniff you out and let yourself laugh with them.

It's not just a game. It's one for the books. Let your inner child thrive again and your dog will thank you for it.

Paws for a Moment

Creating unforgettable memories is reason enough to slow down. Playing like a kid again feels nostalgic and somehow, it feels just right.

Are you just trying to get through the day…or are you creating unforgettable memories in the simple moments?

Day 26: Ancient Ritual

Pawsitive Insight

When your dog turns in a circle before lying down, they're not being cute, they're following a deeply ingrained survival code.

This behavior traces back thousands of years to wild canines who instinctively circled to flatten grass, clear pests, mark territory, and ensure a safe, alert-ready resting space.

Even indoors, on a memory foam bed in a heated apartment, that loop persists. Circling isn't comfort, it's control.

It's your dog scanning, shaping, and claiming the moment before surrendering to stillness.

It's a silent check-in: Am I safe? Is this mine? Can I let go now?

Cute Circle Ceremony

Turn rest into ritual.

Dim the lights. Light a candle. Lay down a blanket like you're preparing sacred ground.

Now sit with your dog. Let them circle. Let them settle.

You do the same, without distraction.

You're not just winding down. You're helping them connect to something ancient, a deep, cellular memory of preparing space before rest.

Paws for a Moment

Peace takes preparation.

A routine for safety. A rhythm of reassurance.

Safety is created, with intention, instinct, and care.

Rest isn't lazy.

It's the most powerful thing you do on purpose.

Day 27: I See You For What You Are

Pawsitive Insight

Dogs are one of the only species on Earth that evolved the ability to read human facial expressions. Over thousands of years, dogs developed this skill through domestication, as the ones who could better understand human emotions had a survival advantage.

Today, dogs can distinguish between happy, sad, angry, and fearful faces, even in unfamiliar people. They instinctively focus on the left side of our face, where emotions are most evident. Every shift in our eyes, mouth, and brow tells them something. This makes your pup an expert in emotion recognition. They didn't just evolve to live with you; they evolved to understand you.

Mirror, Mirror

Sit face-to-face with your pup and exaggerate your facial expressions. I'm talking big smiles, raised eyebrows, silly frowns, and wide eyes. Watch how they react.

Did they tilt their head? Lick their lips? Wag or mimic you?

Keep it playful. Let them read you. Then copy them back and mimic their energy. You're speaking a language without words.

Paws for a Moment

You're always sending signals, even when you're not trying to. A furrowed brow. A tight mouth. A lifted smile that doesn't quite reach your eyes.

The world might miss those things, but your dog doesn't.

They read your face like a page, and they respond without judgment, only presence.

What have you been wearing on your face...

that your heart hasn't had the words to say?

Day 28: Same Time, Same Place

Pawsitive Insight

Dogs thrive on routine because it provides psychological safety. Predictable patterns lower cortisol levels, reduce behavioral issues, and give dogs a stable framework they can trust. Over time, these routines become more than habits. They become emotional anchors. When your dog anticipates their daily walk, or lies down at the same time every night, they're not being robotic, they are self-regulating. The rhythm calms their nervous system. For them, routine isn't repetition. It's reassurance.

THAT'S A WRAP!

After your daily play, create an after-play routine. Use a cue like "All done!" and follow it with a cuddle, a treat, or a cozy walk to their bed. Over time, that little signal becomes something special, not just the end of play, but a gentle promise that you'll be back for more tomorrow..

Paws for a Moment

Your dog doesn't need surprises to feel alive.

They come back to the same corner, the same voice, the same rhythm, and it fills them up.

Not because it's exciting but because it's safe.

What part of your day could feel like peace…if you let it?

Day 29: Till the Very End

Pawsitive Insight

Dogs may live shorter lives, but their bond with us is forever. Research reminds us that to a dog, you are their whole world, and their loyalty usually lasts till the very end. Even as they age, many seniors will still greet you with the same joy as a puppy. They never "outgrow" adoration for you. Their love doesn't wither with time; each gray whisker is simply another stripe of devotion.

Legacy of Love

Think of something to do today that honors everything your dog is. Maybe find a quiet moment to hold them and thank them for choosing you. Take photos of a favorite moment with them, later making a little scrapbook note for yourself. If age or health limits games, try brushing their fur gently while recalling fun memories. This is your chance to pay tribute to the gift that they are.

Paws for a Moment

Time moves faster now. Days blur, routines repeat, and before you know it, everything feels different. But your dog never let that change the way they showed up. Loyalty isn't about doing everything right, it's about staying true, even as life keeps shifting. Through it all, you still know what matters.

Stay loyal to that. Stay loyal to what your heart knows is real.

Day 30: Leave Them With Love

Pawsitive Insight

Dogs are emotionally present creatures. They feel what you're feeling in real time (your stress, your energy, your joy). But what they carry with them after a moment ends is the emotion you gave them last.

Research in canine behavior has found that dogs tend to hold onto the final feeling of an interaction, not the entire sequence. That means if your goodbye was calm and loving, that's what lingers in their memory. If your return was warm, that's what defines the moment.

They don't keep score. They keep feelings.

The Last Word Wins

Pick one daily moment to intentionally end on love. Maybe it's before you leave the house, or when you put your phone down for the night. Get close to your dog, scratch their favorite spot, say something soft, something real. "I love you." "Thank you for being here." "You make everything better." Make the ending matter because to them, it always does.

Paws for a Moment

You don't have to be perfect all day.

You don't have to say the right thing, do the right thing, or feel like the best version of yourself every moment.

But you can choose how you leave a moment.

You can pause. Breathe. Offer love. Not because you got it all right, but because it's who you are at your core.

Your dog doesn't remember every detail.

They remember the feeling.

Leave every moment with love.

Paws for a Moment Final Reflection

You made it. I'm so proud of you.

I bet there were some funny moments, a few surprises, and maybe even a tear or two. But more than anything, I hope this journey brought more love into your life, from your pup, and from yourself.

Because every page was a chance to pause. To become a little more of who you're meant to be.

So as you close this book, take one last moment.

Not to look back — but to look forward.

About the Author

Neal Gyles is the heart behind Paws for a Moment. A creator, dog dad, and a friend for anyone learning how to love themselves again.

This book was born from a deeply personal journey.

After years of struggling with self-identity and feeling completely lost, Neal took a leap of faith to help himself. He dedicated years to personal growth, choosing to fight for his happiness.

Then came Mozzarella, his golden retriever puppy, who transformed that healing journey into something deeper. A new chapter. A new kind of love.

Neal wrote this book because he knows that sometimes, we need to see ourselves through a fresh pair of eyes and a pup's eyes are the purest ones to look through.

To learn more or stay connected, visit:

www.pawsmoment.com

About Mozzarella

Mozzarella is a sweet little golden retriever puppy! She is always so happy and full of life. My heart sings every day when I come home to her. This book is not only a tribute to her entire being but fully inspired by her effect on all the people that she meets and interacts with each day.

Some of her favorite activities include going to the beach and digging up all the sand, spending time on trails in the woods, and bird watching. She has her best friend pups nearby that she sees everyday and she loves kids too.

She shines light in my life and into all of those around her. She is calm. She is happy. She is everything. Her daily life consist of endless love and joy. Mozz has my whole heart, and I could not imagine a life without her.

Acknowledgements

To my younger self —

You would be so proud of what you're up to these days.

You have a beautiful family, wonderful friends, and a puppy you've always dreamed of.

I know there were many times you didn't think you'd even have one. So chin up and keep smiling, little Neal...

You're going to love yourself.

And to you, dear reader —

Take a moment to thank your younger self.

For surviving. For hoping. For holding on.

Tell them: "I'm proud of who you became."

And if you ever feel lost...

You are not alone.

You are so deeply loved.

Dedication

To the dogs that saved us —

for the love they gave so freely.

And to Mozzarella,

my golden retriever,

who reminded me who I am.

Made in the USA
Columbia, SC
06 July 2025